Mosaic

By
L'Travia

Table of Contents

Dedication

This book is dedicated to every soul who has loved deeply, had their heart shattered, picked up those pieces, and has dared to love again. May these pages help guide you to find beauty in the broken places and remind you that there is a light at the end of the tunnel. The best is yet to come, and sometimes the most beautiful pieces of art are the mosaic ones.

Acknowledgment

First, I would like to thank God for giving me the strength to pick up my broken pieces and allowing me to see the beauty in each one of them. At the time, I didn't understand why different things were happening, but I had faith in knowing Jeremiah 29:11.

I've always had a dream to publish a book ever since I was a little girl staying up late reading novels by Mary Higgins Clark, Stephen King, Patricia Cornwell, and poetry by Edgar Allan Poe.

I would like to thank my friends for taking the time to read each poem and give valuable feedback. Thank you for encouraging me to publish my work and letting me know that my poems were worth being heard.

And finally, dear reader, THANK YOU! Thank you for taking a chance on me. I look forward to what's to come.

Choices

Life is made up of nothing but choices.

Each choice affects the next, and if you're not careful, it can become a domino effect.

You may think your choices only affect you,

But trust me, honey, it's just not true.

We're all connected by His grand design,

And God has given us free will because He is kind.

But don't get it twisted, you can still feel His wrath

If you decide to mistreat the ones He's placed on your path.

As for me, I choose the path of love and kindness, peace, and tranquility.

I choose to not let what others do define me.

While others' choices may have broken my heart,

They've still helped to play a major part

In shaping the woman I am today

And for that, "thank you" is what I must say.

I no longer choose to fall in love with people based on their potential.

I choose to see people for who they are, and that choice it's essential.

Each day, choices are made on earth,

And we have got to start choosing better, and know our worth.

Flow

My love for you, it runs deep.

Deep through my veins,

Sometimes driving me insane.

The highs and the lows,

Oh, how you would come and go.

In and out of my life,

On this roller coaster, I see no end in sight.

One day, you're all in, communicating with me,

Asking my schedule so you can plan a time to come see me.

The next day, you pull away and just want to "go with the flow,"

Like my heart is a yo-yo.

When we're together, the times are so good,

Makes me think the off times are just misunderstood.

But I've come to realize

I was not a priority in your eyes.

I was something of mere convenience,

Something to boost your ego and provide you entertainment.

But that's not how I think life should be,

At least not with the romantic partner for me.

I'll cherish the good times we had,

The memories and laughs from the past.

Even though we're apart,

Just know you'll always hold a special place in my heart.

This silence between us is deafening loud,

But this healing journey is making me proud.

Proud of the woman that I am becoming.

Her heart and soul? It's quite stunning.

So no longer will I go with the flow.

I must protect my heart, this much I know.

Healing Journey

Never dim your light for anyone,

Especially someone who's hurt you more times than once.

Whenever someone's actions leaves you in dismay,

Please take to heart what my friends and I say:

"Would your husband treat you this way?"

You are a child of God, created in His image,

And your heart is not to be played in a scrimmage.

Don't let someone's actions destroy your mind,

And always remember, it pays to be kind.

Show yourself some grace and mercy

While you're on your healing journey.

Grief is not a linear process,

It's okay to have a setback while you work through this.

Forgive yourself for what has happened,

Take all of those emotions and tap in.

Tap into the hurt and pain,

Tap into the love and gain.

Gain a deeper perspective on life,

And don't turn into the person holding the knife.

And someday when you're in the mood,

Forgive the ones who hurt you.

Release that pain and all that stress,

And know that your life is eternally blessed.

Sunken place

How I feel, I just don't know anymore,

It's taking every ounce of strength just to get up off the floor.

It takes a lot of guts to finally say, "That's enough,"

And walk away from a family that I was trying to build with you for years.

But majority of it... I've spent spilling tears.

And now I'm sitting here,

Spilling tears again.

I can't even bring myself to put a box together...

Ohhhh we're in another depressive episode again...

Your words cut through my soul like a knife,

Causing your dark eyes to dance with life.

"Go take your crazy pills," you said.

All because I wouldn't let you gaslight me and play with my head.

You left the house with your newfound freedom,

And I called the doctor to ask when I could see them.

The therapist said I should be glad you're gone,

But just last week, she was carrying on and on.

On and on about just how much you love me,

And, "Just give it time, you'll see."

Well, I gave it time, up until this incident

And I wish I could say it was time well spent.

The more time passed, the more it felt like my soul was floating outside of my body,

Watching all of these events unfold.

Slowly but surely, I started to reattach to my body

And took the necessary steps to push depression behind me.

This was no overnight task.

I knew I had to put in work if this healing was going to last.

That type of "love" really did a number on me,

But choosing myself is what truly set me free.

People say this, but I mean it with every fiber of my being,

The next time I fall in love, I really hope it has some real, true meaning.

I don't want this person to be a reminder of you.

I want it to be something, so much more, something true.

That pain and depression nearly took me out

But by the grace of God, I clawed my way out.

Not only was I able to put the box together and get up off the floor.

I was able to turn this heartache and pain into something more.

No longer viewing life from the sunken place

But from a place of peace, provided by God's grace.

Broken Pieces

As I look back over my life, I see the broken china doll I used to be.

Before the doll was thrown against the wall and pieces shattered all over the floor,

By a love that was supposed to be something more.

That doll was shiny, bright, and full of life.

Seeing the best in others and not filled with strife.

But something happened after we said, "I do."

Your mask fell, and well, that kind of changed you.

It wasn't long before I realized you had put me on a shelf like I was some kind of prize.

And be that as it may, I am a prize,

It's just not how you saw me through your eyes.

Through your eyes, I was a play thing, and you got bored.

You sought entertainment and made a move on your checkerboard.

That was the first time you threw me against the wall.

The fragile little china doll.

It took years to put the pieces back together.

By your side, I became weathered.

Once the last piece was placed back in, I still didn't feel like me again.

For that version of me retreated, into her shell so she couldn't be mistreated.

And when I finally let my guard down, here you go and turn around,

Hurling this fragile china doll back into the same old wall.

Pieces even smaller now, the shards of glass all around.

The cuts, scrapes, and pained cries, as I wiped the tears from my eyes.

Realization dawned on me as I took my time and picked up every piece.

Although this china doll has been shattered, I've learned life lessons, and that's all that matters.

Never again will I shrink myself so small so that others can feel big and tall.

It hurts more to hold on than to let go.

Where these life lessons will lead me, heaven only knows.

The pieces are back together again.

It took years of work, but my heart is definitely on the mend.

This healing journey was definitely one to see,

Because I'm finally feeling like me.

That mosaic little china doll, shiny and free.

X

Tears were not something I thought you would ever cause.

You were my best friend, my homie, we used to be thick as thieves.

Deep conversations, laughs, and always able to shoot the breeze.

I wish I could rewind back time, back to the day

Where you mentioned shooting your shot, and instead, I swat it away.

The lines got blurred, and feelings I've had for forever resurfaced,

Deepening with each kiss and interaction between us.

My soul always felt at ease,

And you always felt like home to me.

You were my safe space,

And it is going to be hard to replace.

I can't get wrapped up in what could have been.

I'll just be thankful for the joy we did find within.

I don't regret the time we spent

In all those fleeting moments.

I believe your feelings for me were true in their own special way,

Just know that I still love you, even til this day.

But love is not enough for a relationship to thrive.

It needs respect and honesty to keep it alive.

Man can't live on love alone

And neither can I.

So I'll love you from a distance

And pray you continue to spread your wings and fly.

Full Moon

As I stand here with my toes in the sand,

Admiring the view of where the ocean meets land.

The moon is full and shining bright,

Recharging my soul and restoring my sight.

My vision's been blurred for months on end,

Refusing to come to terms with the circumstances we were in.

Our union is over, that much is clear,

But I can't comprehend.. how did we get here?

How did we get to the place where we have nothing to say?

That doesn't cause pain and dismay?

You love me in your own way, that much is true,

And best believe, I love you too.

But standing here surrounded by nature's beauty

Is allowing me to see that it's time to love me.

It's time to love me enough to know

When it's time to let go.

And while letting go is going to hurt,

Holding on just won't work.

When it comes to this one sided ordeal,

I've had enough, I need something real.

I can't continue to pour from an empty cup,

I deserve a love that's going to fill me up.

Fill me up and not deplete me,

Fill me up and actually see me.

See me for the woman I am,

And who I'm destined to be.

So while I stand here under this full moon, with the waves rolling in around me,

Restoring my soul, causing me to look forward to my destiny.

How you feeling?

If you ask me how I'm feeling,

I'll probably tell you I feel jaded,

Slighted and abandoned by a love I thought I knew.

Who ever thought it would've been you?

You probably think that I'm doing better now,

Life's all sunshine and daisies since you're not around.

But that's only because I know how to straighten my crown,

Hold my head up high and never slump down.

They say love is pain,

But I refuse to believe that that's the kind of love that God
has for me.

So while I might feel slighted, jaded, and abandoned by you,

You only opened the door for a love that's more true.

Truer than hurt, truer than lies,

Truer than disappointment and all the nightly cries.

The cries of my soul reaching out,

Inducing anxiety because of the chaos that's all about.

I'll take quiet and peace and love any day

Over chaos and dysfunction disguised as chemistry, because they don't know the way.

The way to a love so pure and true.

Looking deep within and letting Jesus in

To help mend the brokenness and the pain,

To restore your light and to show you that you have so much to gain.

So ask me again how am I feeling?

I'm feeling restored, refreshed, and renewed.

Remain True

I have no clue where things are going to lead,

But I do know that on the other side will be an even better version of me.

So, like a phoenix, I'll continue to rise.

Rise from the ashes of my heart's demise.

I'll keep loving and giving my all,

But I'll be pickier for whom I fall.

I wish no one ever had to feel this way

But if you do, take heed of my words and be sure to pray.

Pray for deliverance from empty "love".

Pray for strength, peace, and wisdom to discern the truth.

Pray for the ones who have hurt you.

For more times than not, they've been hurt themselves

And now they bleed onto everyone else.

Forgive them, for they know not what they've done.

They didn't know your heart was the precious one.

The one that was sent to give love and heal.

The one that was sent and was the real deal.

So, do yourself a favor and pour that love where it's needed most.

Pour it into yourself and be sure not to boast.

Remain humble and true,

And continue to be the real you.

Love

I've come to the realization that maybe I'm not meant to be loved the way that I show love.

For I will love my partner unconditionally, and I am loyal to a tee.

I will be by his side, forever in stride.

No matter what the seasons may throw our way,

It doesn't matter because God has the final say.

But for some reason, it seems that my very essence,

My light, my soul, may be a little too much for the men that have pursued me.

For the men they claim

They love my light; it draws them to me like a moth to a flame.

Few have had the pleasure to taste my energy

And be treated to somewhat of a jubilee.

A love like mine

Is something you'll experience once in a lifetime.

I'll continue to shine my light very bright,

Who knows, maybe one day it'll attract Mr. Right.

And that one day will be a blessing to see,

The love story that God has in store for me.